Oil has been seeping into the ocean since the days of dinosaurs. Ancient Egyptians used petroleum when preparing mummies for burial. The ancient Chinese pumped gas using bamboo poles, 2,500 years ago. **Native Americans** rubbed oil over their canoes to waterproof them. People in India treated diseases with oil. People in Poland used oil to light lamps 500 years ago, and the Persians have been **excavating** oil for more than 400 years. Still, it wasn't until cars came along and people began using **electricity** to light their houses that the demand for oil really shot up.

Fast Fact

Crude oil and petroleum are both names for unprocessed oil that comes out of the ground, but petroleum may also contain gases and solids.

The more people transported and drilled for oil, the more oil spills there were. Thousands of animals die in oil-polluted waters every year. Millions of tons of crude oil end up in our oceans, rivers, and land. Some of it is from oil spills, some from natural **seepage**, but a lot comes from oil being poured down the drain or oil washing off roads.

Fast Fact

Once, all oil was tiny plants and animals that lived in the sea. When they died, they sank to the bottom of the sea and were covered in mud and sand. Over millions of years, weight, heat, and **bacteria** changed them into oil.

Oily Extractions

When American businessman George Bissell saw a bottle of "rock oil" in a shop for sale as medicine, he picked it up and shook it. "I wonder if this oil could be used to light lamps?" he thought. Not long after that, someone told him about a farm in Pennsylvania that had oil seeping out of the ground. He bought the land, and his company hired Edwin L. Drake and his crew to get the oil out. Drake dug pits with shovels, but it took too much time and effort. One day, George Bissell saw an **advertisement** showing salt being drilled out of the earth. "Hmm, perhaps we could drill oil out, too?" Bissell thought. Drake was thinking the same thing. In the spring of 1859, Drake made a **derrick** and began drilling for oil. He struck "black gold," and soon after, everybody was drilling for oil.

◯ Drake Well, Pennsylvania, 1859

When people first began drilling for the "black gold," it rose to the top in a gush. They drilled holes, called wells, into an oil **reservoir**. The natural pressure of the reservoir, combined with the use of pumps, drove the oil into the well, which then helped bring the oil to the surface. Many wells have other wells drilled next to them, to pump water, steam, acids, or gas down to increase pressure in the reservoir, or to thin the oil. This helps crude oil rise up the production well.

The "black gold," or crude oil, is refined into gasoline, kerosene, and **asphalt**. At first, people bought the kerosene to light their lamps, and then they found other uses for the oil. They mixed the asphalt with sand and gravel for paving roads, and the gasoline was used to power cars and machinery. Some of it was even made into plastic. The more uses people found for oil, the more oil they needed.

Fast Fact

Most easy-to-find oil has already been found and extracted. These days, it's becoming harder to find. If oil companies have to use other materials or expensive equipment to extract and **refine** oil, gasoline and anything that uses it becomes more costly for us.

Oil Tankers

Many countries soon began drilling for oil: from the frozen lands of Alaska to the hot, dry deserts of the Middle East, from small countries such as Norway to large countries such as Russia. Not everyone found oil, though, and what was found wasn't enough. So countries bought oil, and it was transported all around the world in huge ships called "tankers." Over the years, the amount of oil needed increased, and the tankers became bigger and bigger.

Once the tankers off-loaded, or unloaded, their oil, the crew cleaned their cargo tanks and washed the excess oil into the water. They also released their waste engine oil into the ocean.

Sometimes tankers crashed or had accidents on board that would leak millions of gallons of oil. During **World Wars I and II**, hundreds of tankers were bombed. Those ships are still leaking oil from their **hulls,** and the bigger the hull – the bigger the oil spill.

◔ Oil from the *Exxon Valdez* spill

◔ The *Exxon Valdez*

One of the worst oil spills from a tanker happened on March 24, 1989. Shortly after midnight, the *Exxon Valdez* supertanker crashed into Bligh Reef. Eight of its 11 cargo tanks spilled 11 million gallons of oil into the Prince William Sound in Alaska. It took the crew three days to find the cleanup equipment, while the oil spread down the coast. By the time the crew began to clean up the oil slick, it was no longer possible for them to contain it. It killed thousands of birds and other wildlife and destroyed **ecosystems** along the coastline. Years later, animals are still dying because of the harmful effects of that oil spill.

TRY IT YOURSELF!
Like Attracts Like!

Did you know that oil is afraid of water? When there is an oil spill in the ocean, it will stick to animals, sand on beaches, or rocks before it will mix with water. Don't believe it? Then ask an adult to help you try this experiment:

You will need:
- ✓ Food coloring
- ✓ A glass of water
- ✓ Cooking oil
- ✓ A tablespoon
- ✓ A plastic or glass drinking bottle

OIL

RED COLOR

Add a few drops of food coloring to a glass of water. Pour 2 tablespoons of the colored water and 2 tablespoons of cooking oil into a small drink bottle. Screw the lid back on and watch what happens.

Water **molecules** are attracted to each other, and the same is true for oil molecules. They are more attracted to their own molecules than others, so they won't mix together. If you add detergent you will see that it is attracted to both water and oil, helping them all join together.

Oil Platforms

Mexican fisherman Rudesindo Cantarell was mad. Every time he pulled in his shrimp fishing nets they were smeared with oil. He took his nets to the nearest oil company and demanded they buy him new ones. At first they ignored him, but one day they went with him to his fishing spot. They saw the streaks of oil in the Gulf of Mexico. It turned out Cantarell had found one of the largest offshore oil fields in the world. The oil company named it after him. Since 1971, more than 12 billion barrels of oil have been drilled out of the Cantarell oil field.

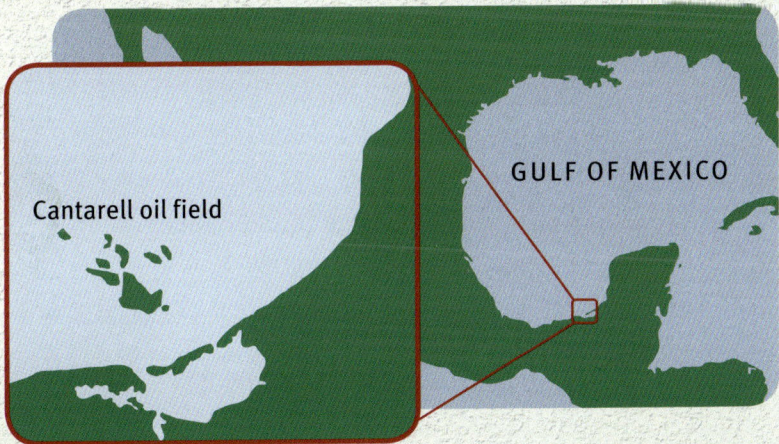

Cantarell oil field

GULF OF MEXICO

Fast Fact

Geologists believe that the circular shape of the Cantarell oil field was made by an asteroid slamming into the Yucatan Peninsula 65 million years ago.

To get oil out of the seabed, a drilling company must build a large drilling platform. In shallow water, platforms are lifted above the waves on legs. In deep water, platforms are supported by large floats, or the drilling rig is built into a big ship. Deep-sea platforms are held in place by large anchors, or sometimes by motors controlled by computers to keep the platform exactly above the hole in the seabed. Platforms generate their own electricity, get rid of their own waste, and are prepared for almost any emergency. They contain living areas and store drinking water, food, and supplies for the crew. The crew live on board for many weeks before taking a break on land.

On April 20, 2010, a crew was going about their night duties on an oil rig in the Gulf of Mexico, when a large explosion blew them off their feet. Eleven workers were tragically killed. A fire sent out large **plumes** of black smoke 30 miles (48 kilometers) long. It took about two days to put the fire out. Not long after that, the oil rig sank. An underwater robot was sent to find out what could have caused the explosion. It found three leaks spewing thousands of barrels of oil a day into the sea.

🔽 The oil rig on fire

The oil company responsible for the spill decided the quickest and easiest way to stop the spread of oil was to set it on fire once it reached the ocean's surface. However, this method only works when there is little or no wind to spread the oil around. Also, only the thinner oil burns, leaving thicker tar to float away.

Two weeks later, a specialist crew made their first attempt to stop the leak. They failed. Five months later, the main leak was finally stopped with a cap that sealed the end of the oil well on the seafloor. The cleanup for this disaster will take many years.

Oily Environments

When an oil spill occurs, it is often carried long distances by **ocean currents**, tides, and strong winds. Sea creatures, as small as **plankton** and as big as whales, can die in oil-polluted waters when they cannot get enough oxygen from the water. The oil burns their skin and eyes. When birds' feathers become coated in oil, they sink and drown. Young fish are born deformed when oil has coated the eggs from which they hatched.

The oil washes up on to beaches and rocks, and into wetlands. People cannot make their living from fishing, children cannot go swimming, and tourists don't want to see oily beaches. All the people living along coastlines are affected in some way when an oil spill happens near them. Some people feel angry with the oil companies, and others are sad because of the destruction. Some people will take action to help clean the environment and save the wildlife.

Two decades after the Gulf War, Kuwait and Saudi Arabia are still suffering the consequences of one of the world's largest oil disasters. At the end of the war, Iraqi troops set 783 oil rigs on fire and sank many oil tankers. Around 11 million barrels of oil were released. Oil spewed into the Persian Gulf, sank into the land, and formed oil lakes in the deserts. The drinking water was polluted, some of the marshes are still dead, and many **habitats** have not recovered.

⊙ Burning oil fields

Cleaning Up

After a spill, a cleanup team will try to control the oil slick to keep it from spreading. They put floating **booms** into the water to surround a slick to make it easier to remove the oil. Sometimes they will use the floating booms to protect areas such as **harbor** entrances. To remove the oil, the team will use skimmers and booms to sweep the oil off the surface of the water. They might also use materials that absorb oil, called **sorbents,** at the final stages of removing oil in the water. In some cases, lots of people with buckets and shovels will join in to help remove tar. They might also use chemicals or high pressure hoses to spray water. If oil has coated solid objects such as rocks, pebbles, or stone beaches, helpers will use steam and scrapers to get the oil off.

⬤ Cleaning up after the *Exxon Valdez* spill

◬ Oil containment boom around New Harbor Island, in the Gulf of Mexico

◬ Floating booms

Fast Fact

Scientists have found bacteria that will eat oil! They were used in the *Exxon Valdez* oil spill but didn't seem to make much of a difference. Now, though, scientists have found bacteria growing naturally in the Gulf of Mexico that seem to have munched through some large oil plumes. The warm waters of the Gulf of Mexico help bacteria grow faster, so they eat oil much quicker than in the cold sea in the Gulf of Alaska.

After the oil spill in the Gulf of Mexico, all zoos and aquariums were put on alert. Sea turtles that washed up on beaches were taken to wildlife centers for care and cleaning. The staff and volunteers used toothbrushes and scrubbing brushes to remove the oil that was caked on turtles. Turtle eggs removed from oil-damaged coastlines were kept in **incubators**. Once they hatched, they were released near the water's edge on oil-free beaches.

Governments in most countries have laws to help prevent oil spills from happening. They make sure oil companies use safe practices. For example, they demand that all underground storage tanks use double linings and that tankers use double hulls to prevent leaks. Drilling companies will often drill sideways so they don't have to dig so many wells.

We can help protect our oceans, too. We can use less oil by walking, riding our bikes, or taking a bus to school. Adults can make sure they do not pour oil down the drain. We can use less power (often generated from oil and gas) in our homes by designing them to be more efficient. We can also turn off lights and computers when we're not using them. If we all pitch in, we can help keep oil out of our oceans.

Rescued pelican released at the Phoenix Zoo ▸

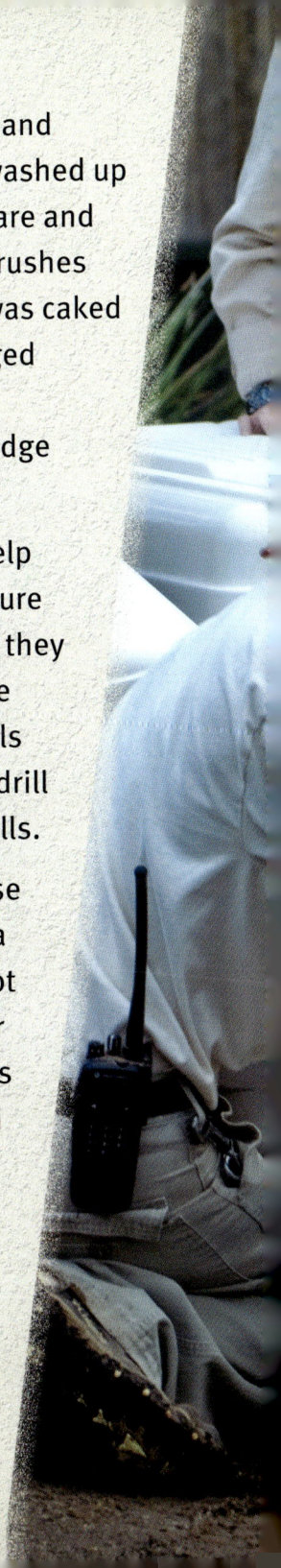

Glossary

advertisement[1] – a commercial, something used to sell a product or service

asphalt – a petroleum product mixed with gravel or sand that is used for paving roads

bacteria – tiny living things (that can't be seen with the eye), some of which eat dead plant and animal material

booms – floating barriers made of plastic or rubber

derrick – a tower built over an oil well that allows drilling equipment to be raised and lowered

ecosystems – communities of living things and the places where they live

electricity[3, 7] – a natural form of energy

excavating – removing something from under the ground

habitats – the natural homes of plants and animals

harbor[6] – an area of water that is deep enough for ships to rest safely

hulls – the frames or bodies of ships

incubators – boxes that use heat to help hatch eggs

molecules – groups of two or more atoms (pieces of matter that cannot be seen with the eye) that stick together

Native Americans[6] – the people living in North and South America before the Europeans arrived, and their descendants who still live there today

ocean currents[3, 7] – movements in the water of oceans

oil[3] – a thick, greasy liquid that doesn't mix with water

plankton – tiny animals and plants that live in the water

plumes – structures or forms that look like long feathers

refine – to take away parts from something in order to make it more pure

reservoir – an area down in the ground where something, such as oil, is contained

seepage – slow spreading into something

sorbents – materials that absorb oil

volunteer[7] – a person who offers to do something for no pay

World Wars I and II[7] – wars that were fought from 1914 to 1918, and from 1939 to 1945

Academic Vocabulary Key	4 Economics	8 US History	12 Technology
1 English Language Arts	5 Civics	9 World History	13 General Arts
2 Mathematics	6 Geography	10 Health	14 Dance/Music
3 Science	7 General History	11 Physical Education	15 Theater/Visual Arts

Oily Beginnings

The wildlife officer knelt in coral-white sand and dug a deep hole until he felt a row of eggs. Before lifting any out, he drew a pencil line on the eggs so he would know which way was "up" when he stored them. Then he picked up an egg with his gloved hand and put it into a container. A **volunteer** packed sand around it. They continued removing eggs from the nest and placing them in containers, making sure the pencil marks on the eggs faced up. Once the nest was empty, they carried the container to a car and drove the turtle eggs hundreds of miles away from the **oil**-soaked coast of Alabama. If left to hatch on this northern Gulf of Mexico beach, the turtles would have swum right into an oily ocean and died.

Fast Fact

The very first oil spill occurred in 1818. Two men digging for salt drilled a hole, and hit a pocket of oil. It gushed out and flooded the Cumberland River in Kentucky.

CSI CHAPTERS

What a Mess!

By Maria Gill

Contents